PREFACE

This book is addressed to teachers in Further and Higher Education, though it is probably equally suitable for nurse tutors, managers, YTS trainers, and others. Teachers in schools, too, may be able to adapt these ideas to their own situation.

The book is the second of a series, each of which suggests practical ways of going about various aspects of teaching. All the suggestions we offer have worked for us or for colleagues: they are all tried and tested ways of doing things. You are probably familiar with some of them already. While there are sound theoretical justifications for these methods (and occasionally even empirical evidence in their support), they are offered here simply as ideas worth trying for yourself. We find them rewarding to use. We hope you find some of them equally rewarding.

This book is not meant to be read from start to finish, but rather to be dipped into. Although the suggestions are grouped together under headings, and are cross-referenced, they are written so that each makes sense on its own. Each one follows a similar pattern: a statement of the problem or issue it addresses, a description of the method and, where this seems helpful, examples of its use and suggestions for dealing with possible difficulties. Where appropriate we have made reference to original sources of ideas or to places where fuller explanations can be found.

Many of the suggestions in this book are based on principles which may be new to your students. If they are not accustomed to taking responsibility for their own learning, for example, or expressing their feelings in the group, they will need time to get used to the idea. When introducing them to a new method, you can help them by telling them what is involved, explaining why you think it's worth doing and giving them time to think about it and talk it through in the group.

If you find the material helpful and you have not already seen the first volume, 53 Interesting Things To Do In Your Lectures, you can obtain it (price £4.00) from
Technical and Educational Services Ltd.,
37 Ravenswood Road
Bristol BS6 6BW

Sue Habeshaw   Bristol Polytechnic
Trevor Habeshaw   Bristol Polytechnic
Graham Gibbs   Oxford Polytechnic

GLOSSARY

There is considerable variation in the meanings which different people ascribe to the terms 'seminar' and 'tutorial'. For the purposes of this book we are adopting the following definitions:

Seminar: a session in which a student presents a prepared paper to the group and is then expected to lead the discussion based on it.

Tutorial: a group discussion, usually chaired by a tutor.

NOTE

Items 8 to 12 in this book apply specifically to the seminar. All the rest of the items are written in terms of the tutorial and are addressed to the tutor, but many of them can equally be applied to the seminar and be used by the student seminar leader.

53 INTERESTING THINGS TO DO IN SEMINARS AND TUTORIALS

by

SUE HABESHAW
Senior Lecturer in the Department of Humanities
at Bristol Polytechnic

TREVOR HABESHAW
Principal Lecturer in the Centre for Educational Services
at Bristol Polytechnic

GRAHAM GIBBS
Principal Lecturer and Head of the Educational Methods Unit
at Oxford Polytechnic

53 INTERESTING THINGS TO DO IN SEMINARS AND TUTORIALS

CONTENTS

I   STARTING OFF

1.   Getting to know you

2.   Learning names

3.   Contracts

4.   Ground rules

5.   Objectives

6.   Orientation

7.   Starting again

and the reason why I'm here is this is the only department that can afford carpets

GETTING TO KNOW YOU

The sooner members of your tutorial group get to know each other, the sooner they will feel easy about working together and participating in discussion. If you spend some time on introductory exercises at the beginning of a course, students will feel that they have made a start in getting to know each other.

There are three sorts of exercise you can do: individual, in pairs, or in small groups. (Whichever you do, don't forget to join in yourself.)

a) __Individual__

Each person introduces herself and says something about herself. It's helpful if you make explicit what this should be and write it on the blackboard. It could be:

- my name
- where I'm from, and
- why I'm here

or,

- my name
- which options I'm doing, and
- who else I know in this room

b) __Pairs__

Group members get into pairs and spend three minutes each finding out about their partner. At the end of the six minutes, each person introduces her partner to the rest of the group and tells them something about her.

One advantage of this type of exercise is that it ensures that everbody has the experience of speaking early on. If you want your students to get used to speaking in tutorials, the sooner they start the better.

c) <u>Small groups</u>

Students form groups of three or four and spend
five minutes finding out what they've got in common
with the others in their group: taste in music; 'A'
levels, Auntie Annies, and so on. At the end of
five minutes they report to the other groups what
they have in common.

If individuals join your tutorial group late, don't forget to
organise introductions for them. You could say, for example,
"This is Chris, who'se transferred from another course. I'd like
to welcome you to this group. Who do you know here ?... Perhaps
the rest of your would like to tell Chris who you are and say
something about yourselves. (I'll draw a plan of the room with
the names on, Chris, to help you remember who everyone is.) And
then we'll ask you to say something about yourself. OK, who'd
like to start ?"

LEARNING NAMES

Members of a group cannot work together successfully if they don't know each others' names. When you meet a new group, find out if they know each other, and if they don't, spend some time working on names.

If you have started with some kind of introductory exercise, they will already have heard each others' names. You can build on this in the following ways:

a) Get students in turn to say the names of everyone in the group and join in yourself. Then change places and do it again until all the names are familiar.

b) On the blackboard draw a plan of the furniture in the room and as students speak, write in each name at the appropriate point on the plan.

c) Ask students to say their own name first when they speak in the group for the first few times and when they form pairs ask them to remind their partner of their name.

d) Encourage them to ask when they forget someone's name.

e) Use students' names yourself when you speak to them.

Students find these activities potentially embarrassing but often remark later how quickly the group gelled as a result.

CONTRACTS

A contract is an agreement between two parties, each of whom undertakes to fulfil his/her side of the bargain in the expectation that the other party will do the same. In educational institutions the situation is less equitable: the details of the students' side of the bargain are usually meticulously specified while the tutors have more flexibility and choice. For example, in most institutions deadlines are set for the submission of students' course work but not for its return by the tutors.

If you want to make the situation more equitable you can negotiate contracts with your students. The first time you meet your tutorial groups you can say,"There are all kinds of regulations governing your behaviour on this course and these are all spelt out in the course handbook. (For instance...) There aren't any regulations for me. I'd like us to spend some time today drawing up a contract which will specify what you expect of me and what I expect of you. Shall we start with a round of suggestions?" **(See 22 ROUNDS).** These suggestions then form the basis for negotiating the contract.

The contract could be, for example, "You will submit your course work by the cut-off date and I will return it to you, marked, within x days of your cut-off date" or "You will do the preparatory reading for each tutorial and I will provide guidelines for each set of reading" or "We all agree to be here at x o'clock each week, ready to start".

Students who haven't entered into contracts before will need to have the concept explained to them and will welcome help in formulating the wording but will have no difficulty in judging what is equitable.

Normally, the very existence of a contract, if it has been freely entered into by both parties, ensures that it will be honoured. If a contract is broken, however, group members need to feel free to remind each other of the contract and feel willing to accept reminders from others. You can aid this by encouragement and by example.

GROUND RULES

All groups have ground rules though usually these are not made
specific. Tutorial groups normally have unspoken ground rules
relating to the role of the tutor (as, for example, "It is the
job of the tutor to devise the tutorial programme, open and
close the tutorials, etc") and ground rules relating to the
behaviour of the students (as, for example, "Students are not
allowed to interupt the tutor though they are allowed to
interrupt other students".) These ground rules are based on
authoritarian teaching methods and actively discourage student
participation.

If, instead of leaving your ground rules unspoken, you give some
time at the beginning of the course to specifying them, you have
the opportunity to ensure that the group has the ground rules
it wants rather than a set of rules based on false assumptions
and traditions.

Students who are unused to setting their own ground rules may
find it difficult at first to see what you mean and will be wary
of making suggestions. They may find it helpful if you take the
activity in two stages: first explain the principle of ground
rules and together make a preliminary list; then, after one or
more tutorials, ask them, in the light of their experience, what
changes they would like to make to the list.

Their list could look something like this:

Ground rules for this group

    (a) No smoking except in coffee breaks
    (b) Don't interrupt other people
    (c) It's OK to opt out and opt in again
    (d) Anyone can suggest changing or adding to the
        ground rules at any time
    (e) Every group member is entitled to time
    (f) It's OK to ask other people for help
    (g) At any point anyone can suggest that the group
        moves on
    (h) We start on the hour and finish at ten to

The best way of ensuring that the ground rules are kept is for group members to be scrupulous from the outset about reminding people when they break them. It is important that you as a teacher don't see yourself as being above the law: you should encourage students to remind you if you break a ground rule and accept the reminder when they do.

See also 3 CONTRACTS.

Some of the activities referred to in other parts of this book have their own ground rules. These are specified where they occur.

OBJECTIVES

Teachers frequently specify their educational objectives for course submissions, prospectuses, etc. These objectives are usually well written and, because they focus on behaviour and skills, give a clearer idea of what is expected of students than can be gained from syllabuses, tutorial programmes or reading lists. So it seems a pity that they are so rarely shown to the students.

If you have already worked out objectives for your courses, it will be a very quick job to make copies of them for your tutorial groups, either on handouts or OHP transparencies. The times when students will probably be most receptive to them will be at the beginning of the course, when they are trying to orientate themselves, and at the end, when they are focusing on the examinations.

ORIENTATION

You and your students come to the tutorial from various other activities and events and from various parts of the building or even from outside. It is probably a week since this group of people met in this place for this purpose. So you need an orientation period. If you start the tutorial before you are all oriented, you will not have your students' full attention and they will not have yours.

The simplest methods of orientation are based on increasing everyone's awareness of the room, the people and the purpose of the tutorial. So it is helpful to spend some time arranging the furniture in the room to suit the group (**see 19 FURNITURE**), putting up posters, writing the programme on the blackboard and so on. If you get to the room first, you can greet the students by name as they arrive. You can spend time chatting about the course with students as you wait for late-comers. And then, at the start of the tutorial, you can orientate students to this week's work by relating it to last week's and to the total programme and quickly running through what you hope will be achieved today. And in time you can encourage students to orientate themselves, maybe by reviewing last week's tutorial with a neighbour or by taking some responsibility for the arrangement of furniture or the drawing up of the programme.

STARTING AGAIN

Students return to courses in two ways: to start the second or third year, or to resume college work after a period of placement.

It can be helpful formally to acknowledge this 'restart' in some way in order to:

a)   bring the group together again as a cohesive unit,

b)   enable any unfinished business from the past to be cleared up, and

c)   signify moving forward to a further stage.

Two examples will illustrate this process:

Rounds (see 22)

a)   One thing I liked about last year was.....
and one thing I didn't like was...........

b)   The best thing about my placement was.....
and the worst thing was..................

c)   I think my performance on the course last year
was..... This year I would like to...........

Pyramids (see 17)

a)   INDIVIDUALLY, students write one list headed 'Good things about my placement', and a similar list of 'Bad things about my placement'. (10 minutes)

b)   IN PAIRS, students show their lists to their neighbours. (5 minutes)

c)   IN FOURS, each person has five minutes to describe her placement, explain what work she did and answer questions from other members of the group. (20 minutes)

d)   PLENARY ROUND: 'The main thing I got from my placement was.....' (This will take one to two minutes per person.)

An additional benefit of this exercise is that it offers some informal feedback to the teacher about the placements.

II   STUDENT-LED SEMINARS

8.   Preparing groups for seminars

9.   Briefing seminar leaders

10.   Supporting seminar leaders

11.   Feedback to seminar leaders

12.   Self and peer evaluation

OK Gerald, we know seminars make you nervous but just how much support do you need?

8

PREPARING GROUPS FOR SEMINARS

When you are embarking on a series of seminars in which students will present papers and lead discussions, you can be very helpful to the group if you spend some time talking about problems of student seminars, organising the programme and identifying what part everyone is to play.

If this is a new venture for the students or if they have had bad experiences in the past, it's a good idea to give them a chance to talk about their worries. A round of "The worst thing that could happen when it's my turn to lead the seminar" (see 22 ROUNDS), followed by the pooling of suggested ways of avoiding these crises, will be reassuring for them.

When organising the programme, you can be helpful to students if you give them the widest possible choice of date and topic. Indeed, this is something you may be able to leave entirely to them. If you give them a list of dates and topics and leave the room (see 32), this will help to accustom them in a small way to making decisions for themselves instead of always deferring to you.

You will need to make it clear to the group that, in a student-led seminar, the immediate responsibility for the session rests with the student leader and that your role will alter correspondingly. If the session is to be a success the members of the group must accept these new roles. This is a difficult adjustment for them to make and they will need help. You could say, "Next week Rosie will be leading the seminar and I shall be a member of the group like anyone else. People will probably find it helpful, Rosie, if you sit here next week, in front of the blackboard where I usually sit. It'll be up to you, Rosie, to decide how the seminar is organised and when to start and finish. How do you feel about that ?" Of course this will only work if during Rosie's seminar you resist all temptations or invitations to take over.

23

9

BRIEFING SEMINAR LEADERS

Students who are to lead a seminar are usually expected to do the preparation for it on their own. If, however, you offer individual students the facility of discussing their seminar with you beforehand, this will give them an opportunity to try out some of their ideas and give you the chance to offer practical suggestions and support.

When they come to see you, they will probably have a fairly clear idea about the content of the seminar but will not have thought about the process. You can be helpful by suggesting that they:

(a)   list their objectives (see 5 OBJECTIVES)

(b)   consider what methods they are going to use to involve the other group members (see, for example, 22 ROUNDS, 24 STUDENTS' QUESTIONS, etc)

(c)   draw up an outline plan for the session to include the methods they are going to use (see, for example, 14 BREAKING UP THE TASK, 13 BREAKING UP THE GROUP) and an estimate of the timing

(d)   list the questions which they intend to put to the group (see 28 OPEN AND CLOSED QUESTIONS). They will find it helpful if they make a list of direct questions, in inverted commas, rather than a list of question topics

(e)   make a copy of any material they want to use as handouts or OHP's.

Time spent at this stage is never wasted.

SUPPORTING SEMINAR LEADERS

A student who is leading a seminar will need your help in adopting and carrying through her new role.

You can help her in specific ways, for example, by sitting in a different seat and letting her sit in the place near the blackboard or OHP and, in particular, by not talking too much yourself. Indeed, you may like to try keeping totally silent for the first half hour, say, or even try staying away from the first seminar altogether to give the group a chance to adapt to student leadership.

If the seminar leader does appeal to you to take over some of the responsibility by asking you when she should start or what she should do next, you can pass the responsibility back gently by saying, "This is your seminar, Rosie. It's up to you ".

If she gets into serious difficulties and dries up or gets totally confused, there are two kinds of help you can give her. The short-term solution, which is humiliating for the student and likely to undermine her confidence for future such occasions, is to take over the seminar yourself. Long-term solutions, which enable her to continue for herself, are to prompt her by saying, "You were talking about 'x' " or, if she has panicked, to say, firmly, "It's OK, Rosie. Carry on". You can talk about this further when you are giving her feedback later (see 11 FEEDBACK TO SEMINAR LEADERS).

FEEDBACK TO SEMINAR LEADERS

Leading a seminar can be a frightening and potentially upsetting experience for students and one in which they often find it difficult to evaluate their own performance. If you set up the opportunity for the seminar leader to evaluate herself and get feedback from the group or from you, the seminar is more likely to be a positive learning experience for her.

If the members of the group feel comfortable with each other, they may give feedback to the seminar leader quite spontaneously without being asked. If they don't, or if their comments are a bit vague ("Very good" or "Well done!"), you will need to set up a structure for them.

One simple structure is the round (see 22) in which all the group members, including the seminar leader and you, say one thing they liked about the seminar. This guarantees positive feedback from everybody in the group and ensures that the comments are fuller and more specific than just "very good". It also gives everyone some extra practice in evaluating.

Another similar structure is **SELF AND PEER EVALUATION** (see next item).

If you decide to give feedback to the seminar leader in a one-to-one session afterwards, be sure to invite her to evaluate herself first: this is not only better for her self-respect but also encourages her to develop skills of self-evaluation, an important prerequisite for improvement. When you give your feedback, don't underestimate how powerful a person you are in her life and be sure to balance negative feedback with at least as much that is positive.

SELF AND PEER EVALUATION

This method can be used in a seminar or in any situation where the group is to give feedback to one of its members.

It consists of a round (see 22) in which everyone, including the seminar leader and the tutor, says one positive thing and one negative thing about the seminar. It is helpful if group members flag what they are saying by beginning, "My positive feedback to you is..." and "My negative feedback to you is..."

There are strict rules for this activity as the situation is a delicate one.

     a)   Ground rules for the group members (see 4 GROUND RULES)

          1. Say one positive and one negative thing.

          2. Do not interrupt anyone else or comment on anyone else's contribution.

     b)   Ground rules for the person whose performance is being evaluated

          1. Evaluate yourself first: say something positive and something negative.

          2. Listen to what is said without replying. (The reason for this is that if you reply you may concentrate on justifying yourself instead of listening to the feedback and selecting from it what is useful to you.)

It is also helpful if one group member writes down what is said.This is so that the subject can listen carefully to each speaker and still have a copy of the comments to look over at her leisure.

III   GROUP WORK

Well, rearranging the furniture has done wonders for group cooperation!

BREAKING UP THE GROUP

However small a group is, there are occasions when it is too big to tackle a particular task effectively. Even a group of two can be too big when faced with a new and complex problem, or a pile of unfamiliar literature. Once a tutorial group has been set up, however, there is a tendency to keep working in that size group whatever is being done.

It can be much more effective to alter the group size according to the task in hand. A group of eight might work best as an eight for pooling ideas and making democratic decisions, in two fours for generating ideas and reacting to proposals, in four twos for detailed work and the trying out of half-formed ideas, and as eight individuals for 'leg work', reading, calculations, etc.

Try to recognise when a group seems to be too big for the task on hand and be bold in proposing smaller working units. This can be invaluable for even very short periods.

You could say, for example, "We seem to be struggling with this plan a bit. Maybe it is too much to take on all at once. There are four main sections to the plan. I suggest that you form four groups of three and take one section each. Section one group here...section two group here...OK? I'll give you five minutes in your groups and see how you progress. Then I'll either give you longer or bring us back together. Remember the question is 'What would be the likely consequences if this plan were to be introduced?'

See also   14 BREAKING UP THE TASK
            15 SUB-GROUPS
            17 PYRAMIDS
            20 REARRANGING THE FURNITURE

BREAKING UP THE TASK

Some topics are so big or abstract or complex that groups have difficulty handling them unless the discussion is structured in some way. A simple way of structuring the discussion is to divide the topic into component parts and distribute them among members of the group. For example, students on a Social Work or Community Nursing course could examine the topic of ageing, or handicap, from the various angles of biology, psychology, sociology, social policy and health education. Or students of history could research separately into different commentators on the Industrial Revolution.

The component parts can be presented in the form of a list of topic sub-headings, questions, problems, quotations, etc. Students choose one item and work on it singly or in pairs for an agreed length of time. The group then comes together and hears the report on each item. Finally the group has an open discussion on the topic as a whole.

It is important that sufficient time is allowed for piecing the topic together again. **Jig-saw**, an alternative name for the method, recognises this.

The advantages of this method over open discussion are not only that the topic is covered more fully but also that all students are bound to participate and the standard of their contributions is likely to be higher because they have had time to think.

Incidentally, this method can serve as a model for structuring material in the writing of essays, notes, etc.

See also 13 BREAKING UP THE GROUP.

SUB-GROUPS

The activities covered in Section III (items 13 to 20) involve dividing your tutorial group into sub-groups. This item describes two specific kinds of sub-group - **buzz and syndicate groups** - and summarises their different uses.

(a) Buzz groups

Buzz groups are pairs or small groups of students who are assigned a task or discussion topic for a limited period (often 5 minutes or less) within the tutorial. The name comes from the noise which is generated when students start talking in buzz groups.

A good moment to suggest **buzz** is when you want all members of your tutorial group to reflect actively on something, particularly in the areas of their personal response or experience. You could say, "Talk with your neighbour for a couple of minutes about where you stand on this ideology" or "Can you think of applications of this principle to your own experience? Get into groups of three and discuss it" or "What do you think of it so far? Tell your neighbour".

This discussion can be sufficient in itself and need not entail any reporting back afterwards.

(b) Syndicate groups

Syndicate groups, or problem centered groups , are small groups of students (4 to 6 is ideal) who are assigned a problem to work on in the tutorial. In the case of a complex problem, an entire session, or several sessions, can be devoted to syndicate group work. Students can be encouraged to use the library and other resources to help them with the problem. The tutor, too, can be available as a resource. On completing the problem, groups report back to the tutor and to the other students.

Working in syndicate groups gives your students the opportunity to try out new ideas and methods in a sub-group where they are confronted with alternative suggestions and receive immediate feedback. Reporting back enables them to compare a range of possible solutions to the problem.

LINE-UP

When doing group work (**see items 13, 14 and 15**), you will probably find from time to time that you need to reorganise the sub-groups so that students mix and work with a range of other people. Line-up is a way of doing this which is more positive than just saying vaguely, "Er, can you get into new groups?" It's also more fun.

In a line-up, students line themselves up across the room according to an agreed criterion and then divide into sub-groups according to their position in the line. You can choose a criterion which is unrelated to the work of the tutorial (darkest to lightest hair colour, tallest to shortest, place of birth, etc.) or one which is related to the work of the tutorial (amount of relevant experience etc.)

You could say, "Before we move onto the next exercise, shall we mix the sub-groups? ... OK, how about a line-up? ... Can you all stand up, please? Let's make a line across the room, facing the window, from the person with the most experience of this topic at that end to the person with the least experience at this end. If you're not sure how your experience compares with other people's, then you'll have to talk to them and find out."

When students have decided where to place themselves in the line, you can choose how they should divide into sub-groups. They can join up with their immediate neighbours, in which case you get groups of similar people together, or you can organise mixed groups: if you have twelve students, for example, and you want four mixed groups of three, you ask the students to number off in fours - 1,2,3,4, 1,2,3,4, 1,2,3,4 - and then all the 1's form a group, all the 2's form a group etc.

Other benefits of this method are that it raises the energy of the group and that, depending on the criteria for line-up that you choose, it offers students a chance to evaluate themselves without feeling threatened.

PYRAMID

The 'pyramid' or 'snowball' method involves students first working alone, then in pairs, then in fours and so on. Normally
after working in fours they join in some form of whole group
activity involving the pooling of their conclusions or
solutions. The method was developed by Andrew Northedge (1) for
use with tutorial groups.

The following example illustrates the type of activity which
lends itself to pyramids. A guide to timing is given in
brackets.

Stage 1: individuals

Students note down some questions of
their own which relate to the tutorial
topic. (5 minutes)
You can judge for yourself which of
your tutorial topics are suitable for
pyramids but some examples might be:
(in Economics) the fall of the pound
against the dollar;
(in Psychology) alternative therapies;
(in Drama) the motivation of Hedda
Gabler.

Stage 2: pairs

Pairs of students try to answer one
another's questions. (10 minutes)

Stage 3: fours

Pairs join together to make fours and,
in the light of their discussion of the
questions, identify general problems
and areas of controversy in the tutorial topic. (20 minutes)

Stage 4: plenary

A representative from each group of
four reports the conclusions of her
four to the group as a whole. These
conclusions can be listed on the board
as a record. (3 minutes for each
representative)

The cumulative structure of the pyramid carries with it a number of benefits: the early individual and paired work gives students the opportunity to try out their ideas on their own and with one other person before risking them with a larger number of people;

the progressive increase in group size means that students are repeatedly confronted with ideas and assumptions which are different from their own;

the graded increase in the complexity of the tasks, where each stage is built on the achievement of the previous stage, makes problems easier to handle.

With this in mind, you need to design your pyramid in such a way that students are doing something different at each stage: if you repeat the same task, they will get bored and feel that they aren't moving forward.

Pyramids for specific purposes are illustrated in:
STARTING AGAIN (7)
GROUP SELF-MONITORING (37)

See also SUB-GROUPS (15)

(1) Northedge A "Learning through Discussion in the Open University" in Teaching at a Distance No 2 1975 pp 10 - 19

18

DEBATE

An important use of the tutorial is as an arena for debate.
Tutors often get students to prepare for tutorials by reading
statements of a variety of viewpoints in a controversial area.
The problem in the tutorial frequently seems to be that in
debating the topic students tend to leave the discussion to a
small number of articulate, confident or aggressive students.

A way of involving all the students is to divide them into as
many sub-groups as there are points of view in the controversial
area and then to get each sub-group to prepare a case for its
viewpoint. The debate itself can be organised quite informally.
For example, you could say to a class of trainee teachers,
"Which of you think that behavioural objectives are a good idea?
OK, would you people like to form a group on this side of the
room and prepare a series of arguments for behavioural
objectives? The rest of you are opposed to behavioural
objectives, then, or aren't convinced? Can you get into a group,
then, and prepare your arguments? In twenty minutes we'll come
together and have the debate. What I shall do is ask each group
in turn to make one statement which the other side will argue
against. So you'll need to prepare your arguments in rank order
of importance. Right, you've got twenty minutes".

Some possible variations, which you can employ when students are
accustomed to this kind of debate, are:

- students speak for a view which they don't agree
with

- students change sides half way through the debate

- students role play a proponent of the view they
support

These have the advantage of further improving students' skills
in argument and enlarging their capacity for understanding the
other person's viewpoint.

19

FURNITURE

The arrangement of furniture in the classroom is probably the single most important factor in determining the success of the tutorial.

Unhelpful arrangements

(a)   If the tutor has a special desk, or a higher or larger chair, or even just a special place, this will give her added status and distance her from the students and will make it highly likely that she will dominate the session.

(b)   If students sit in rows facing the tutor, so that they cannot see one another's faces, this will prevent interaction between them and put all the responsibility for the session onto the tutor.

(c)   If there is too great a distance between the participants, or large obstructions between them, such as large tables, this will make it harder for them to communicate with each other and make it easy for individuals to avoid contributing.

(d)   If the tutor sits in front of the board which is used to display information, she then becomes the focus of attention and "guardian of knowledge".

(e)   If group members sit around a long table or in a long rectangle, especially if the tutor sits at one end, this tends to result in a focussing of attention at that end, and the other end disengaging or starting their own discussion.

Helpful arrangements

(a)   Sit in a circle if at all possible, so that everyone can see and communicate with everyone else, with no seats having special status.

(b)   Think carefully about where you position yourself in relation to the board and leave a gap in front of it, so that any group member can feel free to use it.

(c)   Anticipate the possibility of breaking up into sub-groups for some of the time (see also 13 BREAKING UP THE GROUP, 15 SUB-GROUPS and 20 REARRANGING THE FURNITURE).

(d)   Give sub-groups a physical indentity by seating them together.

20

REARRANGING THE FURNITURE

Just as the arrangement of furniture needs to echo the activity of the group (see **19 FURNITURE**), so the furniture needs to be rearranged when the group activity changes.

For example, if students have been sitting in a circle or round a large table listening to an introductory briefing, they can find it difficult suddenly to engage in group work (see **13 BREAKING UP THE GROUP**) with their immediate neighbours: the change of intellectual demands and change of social relations can be too great to accommodate. The transition will be eased if there is a corresponding alteration in the physical arrangement of the group. This can be achieved by students moving their chairs away from the table and into groups and then returning to the table for the pooling of ideas. If there is space, they can form their sub-groups in another part of the room or even in separate rooms.

Similarly, in a situation where students form two opposing groups, as in a **DEBATE (see 18)**, they can arrange themselves physically face to face in two groups, and then move back into a circle for the follow-up discussion.

IV   ENCOURAGING STUDENTS TO PARTICIPATE

21. Getting students to speak

22. Rounds

23. Gifts

24. Students' questions

25. Students' interests

26. Brainstorm

27. Buzzer

28. Open and closed questions

29. Getting students to stop speaking

Come·on! — it's lovely once you're in!

GETTING STUDENTS TO SPEAK

Tutors often complain that they have difficulty getting students to speak in tutorials and students for their part may regard an invitation to participate as "being picked on". The main reason for this is that tutors and students alike seem to believe that while tutors can require students to read books, write essays and sit examinations, they don't have the right to ask them to speak. Other common reasons for students' reluctance to participate in a tutorial are that they don't know the ground rules (see 4), they are afraid of exposing themselves in public, or simply that they sense that the tutor really wants to do all the talking.

If, however, you really want your students to speak and you believe you have the right to ask them to speak and you are looking for ways of making it easier for them, you could start by discussing expectations and ground rules. Exchange views about how you would like the tutorials to be, tell them about your plans for getting them to speak (see below), and specify any ground rules. For example, students often assume that there is a ground rule that all discussion should be conducted through the chair and that they should apologise if they speak directly to another student. If you want a free ranging discussion, you will need not only to introduce the opposite ground rule - "Anyone is allowed to speak to anyone" - but also demonstrate your support for it by the way you behave. You could emphasise its importance by giving the students some practice straight away. You could say, "I'm aware that because I'm a member of staff, you tend to listen more to what I say and address your remarks to me rather than to others in the group. If you do this, the discussion never really gets off the ground and we waste the benefits of being in a group. So what I'd like to suggest is that I keep silent for the next half hour and you continue the discussion. You know enough about this topic to be able to do that quite easily. I shall sit here quietly but if I think my presence is inhibiting you, I'll leave the room for half an hour (see 32 LEAVE THE ROOM). I'm going to stop speaking now."

Students also tend to assume that the tutor is the only person who is allowed to invite people into the discussion, which is a pity because they often know more about their friends' special knowledge and interests than the tutor does. It's good to hear one student say to another, "You know about this, don't you, Mandy? What was it you were saying yesterday?" You could encourage this by introducing a further ground rule: "Anyone is allowed to bring another person into the discussion".

Exercises which ensure that every student will speak fall into
two categories. One is the type of exercise where students speak
for themselves in turn:

    22 ROUNDS
    24 STUDENTS' QUESTIONS
    12 SELF & PEER EVALUATION

The other is the type where a pair or small group of students
talks together on a topic and then selects one member to act as
rapporteur to the total group:

    15 SUB-GROUPS
    17 PYRAMID
    18 DEBATE

In both types of exercise students have time to think before
exposing themselves to the whole group; in the second type they
also have the opportunity to try out their ideas on one or two
other students before presenting them to everybody.

You will find that when the students have spoken just once in
one of these exercises, they will tend to be more willing to
speak again in later unstructured discussions.

22

ROUNDS

One of the simplest ways of ensuring that all your students will speak in tutorials is to agree that rounds will form part of the regular activities of the group. In a round, everyone in turn, including the tutor, makes a statement, uninterrupted, on a given topic. The topic can be proposed by any member of the group. It can relate to the subject matter of the tutorial or to group processes or to the feelings of the group members and can be planned in advance or devised in response to a situation as it arises.

Ground rules (see 4 GROUND RULES) for rounds are:

- speak in turn, not out of turn
- it's OK to pass
- it's OK to repeat what someone else has already said

Rounds are featured in a number of items in this book. Some examples are:

"My name, where I'm from, and why I'm here"
(see 1 GETTING TO KNOW YOU)

"What I would like to see included in this contract"
(see 3 CONTRACTS)

"I think my performance last year was..This year I'd like to.."
(see 7 STARTING AGAIN)

"The worst thing that could happen when it's my turn to lead the seminar"
(see 8 PREPARING GROUPS FOR SEMINARS)

"My positive feedback to you is...My negative feedback is..."
(see SELF AND PEER EVALUATION)

"What I'm taking away from this tutorial"
(see 44 STUDENTS' NOTES)

"Something good my partner wrote in her essay"
(see 49 ESSAY RETURN)

"What's on top"
(see 50 WHAT'S ON TOP)

"One thing I like about being in this group"
(see 52 PRAISE AND ENCOURAGEMENT)

Advantages of the round are not only that it ensures that everyone speaks but also that it highlights the diversity of contributions and encourages students to learn from one another.

If you are worried that the round may take up too much of your tutorial time, you can, of course, set a time limit on each contribution.

23

GIFTS

The more a student puts into a group, the more she gets out of it. A particular application of this principle is seen in the bringing of tangible gifts to the group. These gifts can vary depending on the course.

You could say to a group of law students, for example, "Illustrations of what we've been talking about crop up in law reports in the newspapers all the time so what I suggest we do is to all bring a cutting from the coming week's papers to the next tutorial and I'll bring one too ".

Or, in an English literature tutorial, you could say, "Next week we're going to start on the poetry of the First World War. Obviously I could bring along my choice of poems for us to work on but I'm sure you have all read war poems which have made an impression on you and I think it would be interesting and give more variety to the tutorial if you all brought a poem of your choice and said a few words about why you chose it. I'll bring one too ". (You can have spares available for students who don't bring gifts of their own but these are not generally needed.)

This kind of activity aids group cohesion and the establishment of a group identity. The students have actively participated in the shaping of the proceedings and feel good because they have given and received gifts.

24

STUDENTS' QUESTIONS

Questions in tutorials are usually asked by tutors. There are several advantages in inviting your students to ask the questions for a change: one is that it gives them more responsibility; another is that the students are in the best position to identify those aspects of the tutorial material which puzzle or interest them, another is that they are gaining practice in a skill which they can then apply to asking questions as they are reading, listening to lectures or revising for exams.

Here are the descriptions of two simple procedures based on students' questions. Begin with everyone in the group, including the tutor, writing down a question based on the tutorial material. (It may be something they don't understand which they want explained or it may be a question to which they know the answer, in an area that interests them.) Then either (a) these are listed on the board and pairs of students select a question, their own or someone else's, to work on and at an agreed time report back to the rest of the group on their conclusions. Or (b) individuals in turn ask their question and chair the discussion which lasts until they feel they have received a satisfactory answer.

25

STUDENTS' INTERESTS

Given the chance, students will express an interest in all sorts
of things more or less related to the course. You can foster
these interests in a number of ways: by showing enthusiasm
yourself, by giving plenty of choice in the selection of seminar
topics and essay titles, and by giving time for individual
students' interests in the tutorials. You could say, for
example, in response to a criticism that something isn't on the
syllabus, "No, that isn't on the syllabus and it's a pity in
some ways. But if you're interested in it, Michael, would you
like some time at the beginning of the next tutorial to talk to
us about it and answer some of our questions ?"

This needn't take a lot of time and is not a suggestion that you
abandon your course to pursue an individual's interests but it
does mean that you are showing respect for your students and may
also suggest to you some ways in which you could extend and
develop your course.

26

BRAINSTORM

This is a very good method for the situation where the aim is to expand people's thinking in an area and look for ideas which might not be arrived at by rational methods. Because it is a situation where anything goes and people are not expected to justify what they say and also because they are stimulated by ideas coming from others, the results are often very creative. This method is particularly appropriate at the beginning of a course or section of a course: if the group surveys the area in the broadest possible way, they have a context into which to fit the detail and there is less likelihood that important items will be omitted.

In brainstorming members of the group group call out suggestions which one member of the group - not necessarily the leader - writes down on a blackboard or flipchart.

The ground rules **(see 4)** for the members are as follows:

> (a) call out suggestions in any order;
> (b) don't explain or justify yor suggestions;
> (c) don't comment on other people's suggestions.
>
> (These ground rules give group members the freedom to express their ideas, even if the aren't sure how they might explain or justify them.)

After an agreed period of time, or when no more suggestions are forthcoming, the group turns its attention to the total list, either accepting it as a statement of a range of possibilities (as in example 1 below) or discussing the items and selecting the most useful (as in example 2 below).

The procedure and ground rules will need to be made clear to the group before you start.

Two examples of the use of brainstorm:

1. "On this nineteenth-century novel course, we'll obviously be picking out different matters of interest from different novels but I think it's helpful if we agree before we start on the range of things we'll be looking out for in any novel that we read. So can we brainstorm this? The title is Things to look out for in a novel" and if you call them out, I'll write them up."

2. "As trainee teachers it's crucial that you know how to evaluate your own teaching and what methods of evaluation you have to chose from. Can we do a brainstorm on <u>Ways I can evaluate my teaching?</u> And then we'll pick out the ones we want to concentrate on."

27

BUZZER

This is based on radio and television panel games where competitors press a buzzer to indicate that they want to speak.

It can be used in a situation where you want students to interrupt a recording or reading because it is full of points which they should be challenging and questioning. You could say, "On this handout is an extract from........ which deals with the topic we've just been discussing and I'm sure you'll find that you don't agree with everything the author says. So what I'm going to do is to start reading the passage aloud and I'd like you to press your buzzer when there is something you want to challenge ".

Students don't actually have a buzzer but they recognise the principle and readily interrupt, either with a verbal statement or, more usually, by saying **"Bzzz!"** Once the interruption has been made, the group can then discuss the criticism more fully.

This activity has the effect of relaxing the group and encouraging participation, partly because it's fun and also because students can interrupt with a **"Bzzz!"** without needing to have formulated their precise criticism. And, perhaps most importantly, they feel free to interrupt precisely because this is an interruption exercise. Using this method also means that the group is following through the article or recording as a joint experience and dealing with the criticisms in context.

28

OPEN AND CLOSED QUESTIONS

Since the most usual method used by a tutor to get students to speak is to ask them questions, it's helpful to know something about types of question and their likely effect.

There are several ways of categorising questions. A simple but useful one is the open/closed dimension which groups questions according to how much scope the student has in answering. A closed question gives the student very little scope: "What is the formula for nitrous oxide ?" or "What was the date of the Battle of Borodino ?" An open question allows more freedom: "How would you suggest we put this hypothesis to the test ?" or "Can you say something about the Battle of Borodino ?"

Both sorts of question are obviously useful and have their place in teaching but the mistake that many tutors make is to suppose that closed questions are easier to answer. It's true that they're usually quicker to answer and depend on lower order skills but in fact students find them more worrying and therefore are less likely to reply. The reason for this is that the answer is usually right or wrong which means that there is a higher risk of being seen to be wrong. So tutors who try to get the tutorial going with a few quick closed questions may effectively silence the students, particularly if they claim that their questions are easy, because then students have more to lose if they get an easy question wrong. A set of open questions, on the other hand, will draw students out.

If, during the orientation period at the start of the tutorial (**see 6 ORIENTATION**), you use open questions in chatting to the students, they are then tuned in to answering open questions even before the tutorial has properly started. Such questions could be "How did you get on with the reading ?" or "What did you think of the lecture ?" or, simply, "How's it going ?"

29

GETTING STUDENTS TO STOP SPEAKING

Highly articulate or garrulous students can be as much of a problem as quiet, reserved ones. The trouble is that such students tend either to intimidate or antagonise the other students and discourage them from joining in. The situation is often complicated by the fact that tutors will encourage such students early on because they are so relieved to have someone in the group who is willing to speak.

There are several possible ways of handling this situation:

a) Distribute the speaking time among the students by using one of the methods where everyone is expected to speak (see 21 GETTING STUDENTS TO SPEAK).

b) When setting up sub-groups (see 15),invite the students to identify themselves as high or low contributors and then suggest that the high contributors work together and the low contributors work together.

c) Set up a situation at the beginning of each tutorial or for half an hour during a tutorial in which nobody speaks for a second time until everyone has spoken once. You will need first to explain to the group why you are doing this: that you have noticed that some people are speaking a lot and some people a little and that you want to try to redress the balance.

d) If you have such a serious problem with an individual that none of the above suggestions work, then you will have to confront her on her own, explain how you feel about her behaviour and ask her to change it, offering your help if she needs it.

V   ENCOURAGING STUDENTS TO TAKE RESPONSIBILITY

30. Distribute group roles

31. Working alone

32. Leave the room

33. Carry on without me

34. Self-help groups

35. No-tutor groups

36. Group grades

Carry on without me.....

DISTRIBUTE GROUP ROLES

One way of encouraging students to take more responsibility for the group without overburdening them is to identify the tasks involved in running a discussion group and assign them to individuals. This sharing of managerial roles can also lessen the social awkwardness involved when peers take charge of a group.

Typical roles could be:

> agenda fixer
> chairperson
> timekeeper
> monitor
> summariser
> note taker

Typical interventions for each role might be:

(a) Agenda fixer: "From what you have said there seem to four main things to discuss: 1, 2, 3, 4. I suggest that we take them in order and start with 1, if that's OK."

(b) Chairperson: "Thanks for that contribution, John. What do you think, Anne?"

(c) Timekeeper: "We've spent about 20 minutes on this point. Shall we move on?"

(d) Monitor: "Kate has spoken very little, John. It might be helpful to Kate if you backed off for a bit."

(e) Summariser: "So it looks as though we're agreed that...."

(f) Note taker: "Hang on, Anne. Can I just get that written down, before we go on?"

31

WORKING ALONE

It is frequently assumed that a discussion session should consist of continuous talk and that working alone is for private study time. Yet giving students - and yourself - the chance to think alone, read alone, tackle a problem alone, etc. can be very valuable for short periods at various stages during a tutorial or seminar, and even during a one-to-one tutorial.

Even one minute of such activity can dramatically improve the subsequent working of the group.

32

LEAVE THE ROOM

Many of the ideas described in this book give the tutor a relatively small role: chairperson, timekeeper, etc. And for at least some of the time the tutor is actually redundant. It can then be quite disruptive to those who are working (on their own or in small groups) if there is someone present who is obviously not working. If the tutor is walking around, observing, even sitting in on small groups, this can be distracting to those who are working. Even sitting quietly out of the way, getting on with other work, can be quite inhibiting to students. The smaller the total size of the group, the more inhibiting this is likely to be.

The solution is simple: leave the room.

If you do leave the room, you will probably find that the level of involvement (and noise) increases almost immediately and when you return that the atmosphere has been busier, more wholehearted and more active than when you left.

But the value of leaving the room is not restricted to structured exercises. Conventional unstructured discussions can often benefit from the tutor leaving the room for part or even all of the time. In a tutorial where you felt that the students would benefit from your leaving the room you might say, for example, "I feel this session isn't going very well and I feel uncomfortable about it. I think I'm saying too much and dominating too much and I don't think this is very helpful to you. What I'm going to do now is leave and let you continue on your own. I suggest that you take one item at a time and proceed as you see fit. Mary and John, could you please act as observers and notice how the session goes, reporting back very briefly to the group when we meet again next week. Thanks. I'll see you then. Goodbye."

Having once taken responsibility for handling their own group, students may afterwards behave more productively and take more initiative in tutor-led groups.

33

CARRY ON WITHOUT ME

This is an extension of **LEAVE THE ROOM** (see previous item).

There are times when tutors are unable to meet their students because they need to attend a conference or meeting, for example, or because they are ill. Often they cancel their seminars and tutorials or, if they don't actually cancel them, they send instructions to the students to "get on with something", which the students interpret as cancellation.

In fact your absence gives the students an excellent opportunity to take more responsibility for their own learning and to have the kind of discussion which your presence might inhibit.

If they are not used to carrying on without you, they will need to be introduced to the idea. In the case of a seminar, there should be no problem: you can say, "We've got a programme planned for the next six weeks with one student taking responsibility for each week. I'd like to emphasise the fact that I don't have to be here for the seminar to take place. I may miss one seminar for a meeting and I'd like to impress upon you the fact that I expect you to carry on without me. How do you feel about that ?"

In the case of a tutorial, you could say, "Over the winter months people get colds and 'flu and it's obviously possible that I might be off sick one day. It would be a terrible waste if you just went away when you found I wasn't there. You could run your own tutorial based on the programme we've arranged for the term or you could discuss the lecture or you could do whatever seemed to be a good idea. Let me ask you now, if you'd got a message this morning saying I wasn't coming in today, what could you have usefully done in the tutorial ?"

The discussion can then lead on to the students making a commitment to carry on without you if you are absent. This commitment could form part of a contract (**see 3**).

34

SELF-HELP GROUPS

One of the limitations imposed on tutorials by both tutors and students is the assumption that they occur only when they are scheduled on the timetable and when the tutor is present. Since, implicitly and explicitly, we value collaborative work so highly, it seems to make sense to encourage students to move beyond this limitation by meeting in self-help groups without staff guidance and outside scheduled tutorial time.

A self-help group can consist of all the members of your tutorial group or of a sub-group, or sub-groups within it.

If you introduce your students to the idea of self-help groups, you will find that some of them respond positively and may even be already operating an informal system of self help. Others, who have been influenced by the emphasis on secrecy and competition in traditional education, will be less enthusiastic and will need to be reassured about cheating and plagiarism.

How they spend their time in the self-help sessions is, of course, up to the students, though you can be helpful in various ways when they first set up their groups. You can recommend procedures for the group such as:

(a)   when the group meets, members agree a rough agenda, and timetable, and a time to finish;

(b)   when a meeting finishes, members do not leave without fixing a time and place for the next meeting;

(c)   the group chooses a 'secretary' who takes responsibility for (a) and (b).

You can suggest suitable activities for the group, such as: reading one another's essays, exchanging views about set books, comparing lecture notes, and generally trying out their ideas, and giving one another support and encouragement. You can also help with practical arrangements, such as room booking, and give support generally by showing an interest in the progress of the group.

The likely benefits to students from belonging to a self-help group are an increase in confidence and autonomy and the building of collaborative relationships.

35

NO-TUTOR GROUPS

If the main problem in tutorials is that tutors dominate the group and inhibit the students, then the simplest solution seems to be the introduction of no-tutor groups. If the tutor is not there, then students must take responsibility for the session and for their own learning.

If you want to try this with your students, you will need to explain to them what you expect of them and why you are apparently proposing to abandon them. They will need time to think about it and talk it through. You can ask them to consider, for example, what they think they are capable of achieving on their own and what problems they might expect to encounter. Points arising from this discussion could form the basis for decisions about how to proceed.

Tutors who have tried no-tutor groups have devised support systems and safeguards which you can use if you feel your students need them. You can, for example, arrange to be available for consultation by students during tutorial time. Or you can support your students in your absence by providing them with structured exercises and programmes. You can maintain contact with what goes on by meeting with them once every three or four weeks and by requiring them to keep written records or tape-recordings of their sessions. If you prefer, you can maintain closer contact by alternating no-tutor and tutor groups so that your students can ask you to help with unresolved problems before too much time has elapsed. When they get used to making decisions for themselves, you can ask them to decide what kind of support they want from you.

Experience shows that if you introduce no-tutor groups early in the course, before students have got into the habit of being passive, they are more likely to be a success.

36

GROUP GRADES

Many tutors would like to encourage co-operation and teamwork by getting their students to do group projects but feel hampered by the problem of assessment: they are afraid that, if they award separate grades to individual members of the group, not only will they have difficulty judging individual contributions but also by differentiating between students they will threaten the trust and co-operation in the group.

The alternative, of giving the same grade to every member of the group, often strikes students as being unfair: the hard workers feel that the lazy members are bringing down the standard of the group and taking advantage of others.

A working compromise is to award a group grade which the students divide up among themselves. For example, a group of 6 students may produce a group project report which gains a mark of 62 per cent. The group is then given 62 x 6 marks = 372 marks to divide up between its members as it sees fit.

The advantages of this method are that the marks are being allocated by those who are in the best position to judge individual contributions and that students are taking responsibility for decisions affecting their team. The group may of course decide to divide up the marks equally whatever happens; this is their decision and they are likely to learn from it.

VI   EVALUATING THE WORK OF THE GROUP

Well, what do you think of it so far?

37

GROUP SELF-MONITORING

Students usually know when things are going badly in a group. And they are normally in a better position than the tutor to identify the causes. What they generally lack is some kind of procedure for dealing with the situation.

Tutors in various institutions have developed questionnaires to help students monitor the working of their groups. There is a wide range of these but the simplest and most flexible consists of two sheets of paper which are blank except for the headings **"What's going wrong in this group?"** and **"What's going right in this group?"** Students write their own answers to the two questions and then the group uses this material as the basis for discussion.

A more structured way of using these question sheets is the pyramid (see 17). The stages of the pyramid could be:

(a)   individuals write answers to the questions

(b)   pairs compare answers and identify problem areas

(c)   groups of four discuss possible solutions

(d)   the representative from each group of four presents proposals to the total group

(e)   the total group selects proposals

(An example may be useful here. Students may feel, for instance, that there are cliques within the group and that this is causing feelings of exclusion and resentment. They may decide that the answer is for group members to sit in a different place for each tutorial.)

Group self-monitoring need not take place during tutorial time, or with the tutor present. You could encourage students to run the exercise themselves and take responsibility for their own group. If, however, their recommendations for improvement involve you, you need to be receptive to their ideas and serious in giving consideration to their suggestions.

The value of expending time and effort on this exercise will depend partly on how long the group is to stay together, though individuals can carry forward into new groups the benefits of increased awareness of group dynamics.

38

OBSERVERS

An observer's view of a situation is usually quite different from those of participants in that situation. The observer's view tends to be broader, more selective and more objective. It is worthwhile getting one or two members of your tutorial group to act as observers of their fellow students on occasions when this kind of overview would be useful.

The kind of tutorial which lends itself to this treatment is one which is operating at two clearly distinct levels: at the level of the particular, group members may be discussing the details of a case or an example or an artefact; at a more general level, their discussion is based on principles, theories, criteria, issues, etc., of which they may not be aware. Observers, by remaining apart, are in a good position to extract these broader aspects from the discussion and feed them back to the group.

The observers will probably find it easier to carry out their role if they position themselves physically apart from the rest of the group and make notes, perhaps on a flipchart sheet, as the discussion proceeds. It is important that you agree a clear title for their notes so that the know exactly what they are to look out for. Such a title might be

"General principles which underpin the discussion" or

"Criteria on which the group bases its decisions" or

"Issues arising from the case study".

As an alternative, you can tape record your tutorial and then play the recording to the group, all of whom will act as observers. This has the advantage that it gives everyone practice in developing observer skills. (See also 40 TAPE RECORD YOUR TUTORIAL.)

39

CHECKING IT OUT

Tutors are often heard to make comments about groups of their students like "They find it very difficult" or "I don't know how to get their interest" or "It's not going as well as last year". Usually these comments are well founded in the sense that when the tutor feels that something is wrong, something generally is: the signs of discontent are not hard to read. But the mistake that tutors often make is to expect to be able to judge exactly what is wrong without actually checking it out with the students themselves and asking them. These tutors run the risk of mistaking students' exhaustion for boredom, puzzlement for hostility, thoughtfulness for laziness, and so on.

There are various ways in which you can check things out with your students. For example, if you want to get some quick feedback about your tutorials you can say, "I'm feeling a bit unclear about what you think about the tutorials so far this term. So I'd like to suggest that we go round and everyone says one positive and one negative thing - one thing you've liked and one thing you haven't. I'll start, to show you what I mean" (see 22 ROUNDS). Or, in a less structured form, "I'm worried about the work we've done so far this term in this group. I feel I'm not getting through to you. How do you feel about it?" If your students are likely to be afraid to take individual responsibility for this kind of feedback, they can have five minutes' discussion in groups of two or three and appoint a spokesperson to speak on behalf of each group.

If in a tutorial you ask a question and nobody answers, you can gloss over the fact by answering it yourself or by asking a further question or, better, you can check out why the students didn't answer. You can say, "Nobody's answering the question. Is that because it isn't a very good question?" and if still nobody answers, "Marianne, would you like to say something about this?"

Checking it out with individuals can also be very helpful - and revealing. You might say, for instance, "You look fed up today, Simon. Are you?" or "You look puzzled, Paul. Can I help?" or "You look as if you've just had a good idea, Hayley. Can we hear it?"

40

TAPE RECORD YOUR TUTORIAL

If you want to review or analyse some aspect of your tutorial - to calculate how much time you spend speaking compared with the students, for example, or to see how long those silences really are - or if you just want to see what the tutorial looks like from outside, you can make a videotape of it.

The best results are obtained from using two cameras, in which case you will need someone in the room operating the equipment for you. Alternatively, you can use one fixed camera, which is fine for a small group and is less intrusive because nobody is needed to operate it. Least threatening of all is the sound tape recorder but of course if you have sound only, you miss everything that is to be learned from seeing the body language of the group. You can, however, get a long way with very simple equipment. Your audiovisual unit will probably be keen to set it up for you.

Before you start you should explain to the group your reasons for making the recording and you should show them the tape afterwards. Indeed, you will get far more value from it if you watch it with them and ask for their comments. At first, of course, they will be interested mainly in seeing themselves on television but when they get used to that, they will be able to give you useful feedback on their perceptions of the tutorial.

The type of feedback you want will depend on your reasons for making the recording in the first place but these are some structured exercises with general applicability:

(a)   The group watches the tape and then each student suggests one thing you could do to improve the tutorial and one thing she could do. These suggestions can be spoken or written.

(b)   Play the tape, stop it at an important point (e.g. at a point where you asked a question and were met by silence) and then ask all the students to say what they were thinking at that moment and tell them what you were thinking.

(c)   The group watches the tape. Any participant can stop it and recall what was significant for her at that point. The difference between this and (b), above, is that here the stop button is controlled by the students, who are in the best position to judge where in the tutorial things went right or wrong.

(d)   Play the tape and get pairs of students to analyse different aspects of the tutorial such as body language, how many times each group member spoke, evidence of objectives, types of question asked (see 28 OPEN AND CLOSED QUESTIONS), etc.

These exercises need not be too time consuming. You don't have to watch the recording of the whole tutorial. The first few minutes are in fact often the most important and revealing.

41

CONSULTING THE GROUP

Tutors often have the experience of feeling unsure what to do, even in a carefully planned tutorial, either because time is running out or because there is a choice of directions which the group could take or because something unexpected happens. Usually, however, they try to conceal this uncertainty from the students: they make a quick unilateral decision about how to proceed and carry on as if nothing has happened. If, instead, they consulted the group, they would have the benefit of the views of those people who are in the best position to advise.

If you want to consult your group at a time like this, you could say, "We seem to have taken longer that I anticipated so far. I had planned to do x and y as well. There's probably only time for one of them. Which shall we do?"

After students have got used to taking some responsibility in this way, they are likely to start suggesting courses of action, and alternatives to those you suggest. For example, in response to the above question, they might say, "Neither, thanks. We'd like to spend the rest of the time discussing what we've done so far".

Once you have established this kind of student involvement, you can design your sessions in a much more open-ended and flexible way, and spend less time worrying about them beforehand.

VII   WRITTEN MATERIAL

42. Display
43. Group charts
44. Students' notes
45. Handouts
46. Writing
47. Open-book tutorials
48. Essay preparation
49. Essay return

He lost a whole term's prepared lectures when a gerbil made its nest inside his word processor

DISPLAY

Blackboards, whiteboards and overhead projectors are frequently used in lectures to display material and can be very helpful to students: even a few words or a simple diagram can clarify anything from simple spellings to complex concepts and relationships.

Displaying verbal or visual material can be equally helpful in tutorials. You can display your objectives (see 5), the agenda, an ongoing summary of the discussion or a set of headings to serve as the basis for the students' own notes. This not only clarifies things generally but also gives an opportunity for those who get left behind to catch up. At the simplest level, if students can see how unfamiliar words and names are spelt, they will feel more confident about using them and looking them up in indexes and library catalogues.

One reason why tutors tend not to display material in tutorials seems to be that they feel that the use of a board is too formal for what is a relatively informal teaching situation. If you feel too authoritarian with a piece of chalk in your hand, consider bringing your students into the activity (see also 19 FURNITURE). You could say, "That's a good idea, Louise. Would you like to add it to the list on the board?" or "That'll be a new word to people in the group, Dave. Can you write it up on the board for us, please?"

See also **43 GROUP CHARTS**.

43

GROUP CHARTS

It's always interesting to experiment with presenting material visually. Many students will find it easier to understand a concept or model or set of relationships if you present it in the form of a diagram. The notion of the group chart is a particular application of this and is based on the technique of patterned note taking developed by Tony Buzan (1).

Patterned or organic notes begin with a central idea in the middle of the page and work outwards along lines of association. The material is organised on the page according to links, contrasts, groupings and parallels. These can be emphasised by means of arrows and other symbols, by varying the thickness of the lines and by the use of different coloured pens. An example of a set of patterned notes is given overleaf.

This method, which some of your students probably already use for their personal notes, can be adapted for use by the group as a whole. You can begin by writing the theme of the tutorial in the middle of the board or of a sheet of flip chart paper and then invite individuals to add the lines of association as these arise in discussion. For example, in the illustration overleaf, the chart began with the central theme of "non-verbal communication" and students who introduced the areas of "books", "benefits", "dangers", etc. added them to the chart. For people who have worked on such a chart and explored the relationships within it, this method of presenting material is much more meaningful than a simple list of items would be. It also serves as a model for students when they are assembling ideas for essays.

Writing on flip chart sheets rather than on the board, means that when a theme continues over more than one week, the students can carry on where they left off and also that you can store all the charts and display them for revision purposes at the end of the course.

(1)   Buzan T Use Your Head BBC 1974

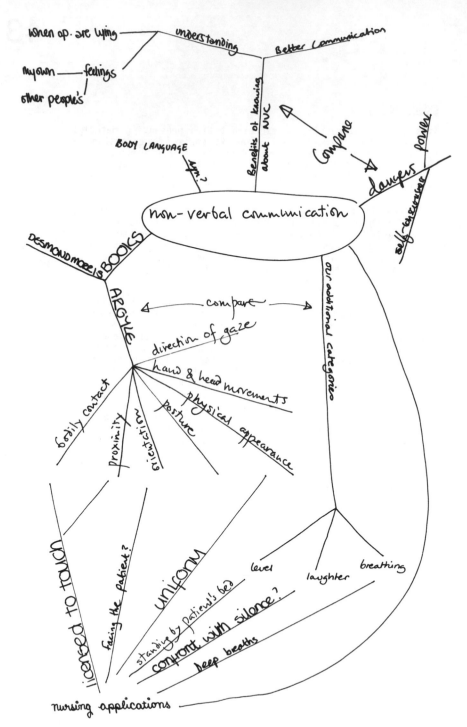

when op. are lying — understanding — Better Communication

my own — feelings
other people's

BODY LANGUAGE

Benefits of knowing about NVC

compare

dangers — power

self-awareness

non-verbal communication

DESMOND MORRIS — BOOKS

ARGYLE

compare

direction of gaze

hand & head movements

physical appearance

posture

bodily contact

proximity

orientation

our additional categories

licensed to touch

facing the patient?

UNIFORM

standing by patient's bed

level

laughter

breathing

confront with silence?

deep breaths

nursing applications

44

STUDENTS' NOTES

It is even more difficult for students to take notes in seminars and tutorials than in lectures. The main problems are that it is virtually impossible to participate in a discussion at the same time as keeping a written record of it and also that it is very difficult in a free-ranging and loosely constructed discussion to keep track of the main arguments.

You can help your students with their notes in a number of ways:

a) Acknowledge that there's a problem and encourage them to discuss it and suggest solutions for themselves.

b) Where a seminar or tutorial has a predetermined structure, indicate this on a chart or handout.

c) Be generous with handouts. Give students copies of references, quotations, questions, diagrams or calculations (see 45 HANDOUTS).

d) Encourage students to interrupt the discussion in order to ask for clarification or time to note things down.

either e) Summarise what is said or get one of the students to summarise, either at the end or at selected points during the tutorial.

or f) At the end of the tutorial get everyone to write down "The three most important things in today's tutorial" and write three yourself. These can be listed on the blackboard and form the basis of students' notes.

or g) Do a round of "What I'm taking away from this tutorial" (see 22 ROUNDS). These contributions, again, can be listed on the blackboard and students can be given five minutes to copy them down.

45

HANDOUTS

Handouts tend to be under-used in the teaching of groups, which is a pity because they can be very helpful in indicating structures and serving as a focal point for discussion as well as saving students the unrewarding labour of copying quotations, etc.

Handouts can contain any of the following:

a) lists or charts of the material or activities to be covered in the course as a whole or in particular tutorials;

b) a list of references which students are to follow up;

c) a passage or set of quotations to be discussed;

d) a set of opposing arguments to be debated (see 18 DEBATE);

e) a set of questions with spaces in which students write answers;

f) a set of headings with numbers for students to list points:

Advantages	Disadvantages
1...................	1...............
2...................	2...............
3...................	3...............

g) a summary of the previous week's session. (Where this was a student-led seminar, the student concerned can write the summary.)

h) problems or calculations.

46

WRITING

Apart from any notes they may take, students tend to do very little writing in tutorials. And tutors tend not to encourage them to write, possibly because writing is slower than speaking and tutorial time is precious. But if you leave writing off your agenda, not only does this restrict the scope of the tutorial, but also it contradicts the emphasis which is placed on written work when it comes to assessment.

This is not a recommendation that students write instead of speaking but that writing becomes one of the range of regular ways in which they express themselves. It seems to work particularly well at the start of the tutorial because it helps students to gather their thoughts and sort out their ideas before engaging in open discussion. If you join in yourself, both you and your students will get more out of it.

<u>Some ways of using writing in tutorials:</u>

(a)   **Key words**

Everyone writes down an agreed number of key words (say 6, or 10) on the tutorial topic. The tutorial agenda can then be derived from the total list. You can start, for example, by writing all the key words on the board and then rank them in order of importance or group them according to common characteristics.

Advantages of this method are that it generates a lot of material from the group in a short time, it focuses people's attention on the essentials, and it provides a useful basis for later revision.

(b)   **Write before you speak**

You ask students the kind of question you would ordinarily ask in a tutorial but everyone writes down their response rather than saying it.

The advantage of this method is that all students have time to work out their answers and have something concrete to contribute to the discussion.

(c)   Pass it round

Everyone writes something on a topic or
in answer to a question. After an
agreed time they pass their papers
round and make notes on each other's
contributions. These notes then form
the basis for the discussion.
This method is suitable for a situation
where you want to illustrate the
variety of viewpoints or angles repre-
sented in the tutorial group.

The timing of these exercises is important. The amount of time
that students need will obviously vary according to the topic,
the size of the group, the individuals in the group, etc. but as
a general guide, the writing part of the exercises described
above will probably take (a) 5 minutes (b) 10 minutes and (c) 10
+ 30 = 40 minutes. You will need to organise the session in such
a way that there is enough time both for writing and for
discussion.

Some students may be hesitant about commiting their ideas to
paper. You can help to reduce such hesitation by:

1.   making it clear that all writing in the
          early stages will be 'private' (e.g.
          between pairs of students);

2.   basing writing tasks on personal views
          or experience rather than specialist
          knowledge which can be judged to be
          right or wrong (see 28 OPEN AND CLOSED
          QUESTIONS);

3.   accepting whatever is written as a
          contribution to the group, no matter
          how unsophisticated it may seem to be;

4.   using writing frequently as a means of
          direct communication rather than only
          when students are assessed.

47

OPEN BOOK TUTORIALS

One reason why tutors are often met by silences when they ask questions in tutorials is that students have quite simply forgotten what they are supposed to have learned from lectures and books.

If your students seem to forget things easily and you don't want the success of your tutorials to depend on their memories, you could try open book tutorials. The name comes from open book examinations, which are sometimes held in such subjects as English literature. Candidates are allowed to use their text-books in the examination room, on the grounds that they are being tested on their critical and analytic skills rather than on their ability to memorise material.

A tutorial in which you encourage students to refer to books and notes will have a different focus in that students' initial response to your questions will be to start turning over pages and reading. But because students will not be spending their time anxiously trying to remember the written material, the atmosphere will be more relaxed and the level of thinking and discussion will be higher.

48

ESSAY PREPARATION

If writing essays is to be a learning experience, students should not have to wait until the essay is returned to discover that they have made fundamental errors at the planning stage. Many tutors are aware of this and one way in which they try to ensure that students are working within a useful framework is by telling them what the framework should be. There are two disadvantages in this method: one is that the tutor is doing the work for the students and the other is that the method doesn't allow for the great variation in students' approaches to the task.

If you want to use some tutorial time for essay preparation, a way of involving all members of the group and benefitting from the variety of approaches is to get students to make a plan for the essay individually and then share their ideas. This sharing can be done by each group member in turn holding up his/her plan and explaining it. (If the group is too large this can be done in sub-groups.) Or, as an alternative, group members can pair off, read each other's plan and then do a round (see 22) of "What I liked about my neighbour's plan" or "How I would summarise my neighbour's plan".

If your students are worried about other people stealing their best ideas, you can get them to do this exercise with non-assessed essay questions or past examination questions until they get used to sharing.

49

ESSAY RETURN

Tutorials are often used to return marked essays to students. This is an economical use of time, particularly if the group was set just one or two essay titles, because there are always some criticisms to be made which apply to all or most of the essays. The trouble is that a common way in which tutors choose to run the session is to sit and make a speech about the essays. This does not take account of the variety and individuality of the essays or take advantage of the potential of the group.

An alternative is the one-to-one tutorial. The advantage of this method is that you are able to give individual feedback to each student. The disadvantages are that it is often unnecessarily time-consuming in that you probably find yourself saying the same thing repeatedly to different students and that you are discouraging students from learning from each other's essays.

The best plan seems to be to use some of the group tutorial time for the return of essays and then to suggest to students some follow-up activities for later.

A group activity which fosters variety and individuality is the round (see 22). For example, students can form pairs and read each other's essays and then do a round of "Something good my partner wrote in her essay". This is good for morale because everyone has written **something** which is good, it contradicts the secrecy which usually surrounds the return of essays, and it illustrates how much students can learn from each other.

You can then add any general comments of your own that have not been covered by the students themselves. (There shouldn't be very many of these if the students have been given enough time and encouragement to do their part of the job well.)

You can follow this up in a variety of ways:

    a)   Make a photocopy of the best essay and give it to the students to pass round after the tutorial. The rationale for this is that if students see what an 'A' grade essay looks like, they will be in a better position to criticise their own work and have a better idea of which direction they need to take in order to make progress.

b) Encourage your students to form self-help groups (see 34) outside class contact hours so that the can read and comment on one another's essays (or, indeed, develop any other study skills).

c) Invite your students to come for individual tutorials with you later in the week when they can talk about matters which relate specifically to their own essays.

VIII   EXPRESSING FEELINGS

50. What's on top

51. Self disclosure

52. Praise and encouragement

53. Concluding

What I want to say is: even though I can't stand Kirkegaard— I really _love_ belonging to this group!

WHAT'S ON TOP?

The substantive topic of a tutorial is not the only thing on the minds of group members, nor necessarily the most important. It can be very useful to have a round (see 22) at the start of a tutorial to allow group members to share those thoughts and feelings which are on their minds: something hanging over from the previous week, the experience of reading an exciting book, telling the others about a TV documentary relevant to the course, or simply saying, "I've got a cold, so I may not be too quick this afternoon". These brief offerings may or may not be very important or interesting to other members of the group but will preoccupy the person involved for the whole of the tutorial unless they are expressed early on.

With in-service groups of teachers, managers, nurses, etc. who are meeting in a learning group in the context of continuing work and professional practice, the opportunity to express what's "on top" may be an excellent way of linking the course with their work. If group members know they will have the opportunity to share experiences and feelings in this way, they are more likely to notice things at work and store them up for the start of the next group meeting. Sometimes, in fact, "What's on Top?" becomes the most important part of the group's activities.

If you are worried that too much of your tutorial time will be taken up in this way, you can of course set a time limit of one or two minutes on each member's contribution.

51

SELF DISCLOSURE

Students get a lot of help and encouragement from tutors' self disclosure. Probably the two most helpful things that tutors can do as self disclosure are to express their feelings and admit to their limitations.

If as a tutor you have a strong feeling about something and you don't express it verbally, it will be a distraction both to you and to your students. If you do express it, this will help to dispel the feeling and also serve as an example which your students can follow when expressing their feelings themselves. Indeed, it hardly seems fair to ask students to do things which you are not prepared to do yourself.

Admitting to their limitations is something which many tutors strenuously avoid. They think that if they show what they imagine to be weakness, their students will lose faith in them. In fact, students have no trouble recognising cover-ups and show respect for tutors who are honest and don't pretend to be perfect. Ways in which you can admit to your limitations are to say, "I'm sorry. I don't understand that" or "I don't know the answer to that question" or "I haven't read that book. Who wrote it?" or "Yes, I get worried about that sort of thing too". And a simple practical favour you can do your students is to show them a rough draft of something you've written complete with crossings out and alterations; they will find it very comforting.

52

PRAISE AND ENCOURAGEMENT

Teachers can often be heard talking about their students and saying how much they've learned from individuals, how nice a particular group is, how well their students work, etc. but these views are rarely expressed to the students themselves. This is a pity because groups work together more harmoniously and produce better results when the members feel good about themselves.

It is a good idea to look for opportunities to give praise and encouragement to your groups, particularly if you characteristically spend time in tutorials criticising and correcting students' contributions. If you are pleased with how they are getting on, say so. You could say, "We're making a lot of progress on this course" or "I think you've worked really well today" or "What we've been doing this morning has been quite tricky so you've done well to keep at it and not give up". If you feel that you can't honestly praise the whole session, then you could say, "We've had our problems this afternoon but I really liked the way you tackled x". There is always something positive you can find to say once you start looking.

If you want to involve the students themselves in this positive thinking about the group, you can suggest that they make a list of "what we've achieved this term" or "what we like about being in this group" or "six good ideas we've had in this group", etc.

53

CONCLUDING

During the academic year tutors and students may spend upwards of 100 hours in each other's company in what is both an academic and a social experience.

A formal conclusion to this joint experience can serve important academic functions: you and your students can draw together themes covered in earlier weeks, state conclusions and reflect knowledgeably upon issues which the course has raised. If there is a post-course examination this concluding session can be particularly valuable for helping students with their revision if some question and answer time is included.

A formal conclusion can also serve important social functions to do with bringing the formal working relationship to an end. This is an opportunity for the group to break up in a positive atmosphere with any loose ends tied up and to express good fellowship and exchange good wishes for the future.

You could introduce this session as follows and lead on to a round (see 22):

"Since this is the last session it would be nice to finish in a positive way so let's all say one good thing we'll remember about being in this group this year. I'll say one too. Who'd like to start?